NAME OF THE SHIP:

___

DATES:

___

ROUTE:

___

THIS CRUISE LOG BOOK BELONGS TO:

___

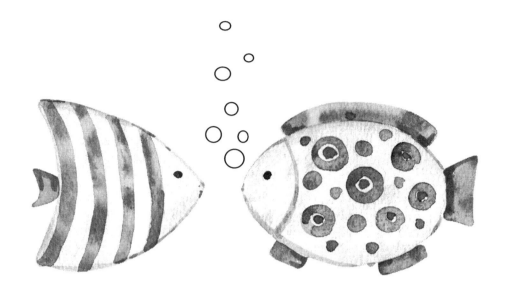

THINGS I HAVE TO DO BEFORE MY CRUISE STARTS

THINGS I WANT TO TAKE WITH ME

THINGS I WANT TO TAKE WITH ME

Date _____

At Sea ○   Port ○   _____

Weather ☀ ☁ ☂ ❄   Temperature _____

	Restaurant	Menu Choice
Breakfast		
Lunch		
Dinner		

Shipboard Activities

Excursion

Evening events _____

Attire _____

Favorite Memory _____

New Friends _____

Don't forget! _____

THINGS I WANT TO REMEMBER

Date _____

At Sea ○ Port ○ _____

Weather ☀ ☁ ☂ ❄   Temperature _____

	Restaurant	Menu Choice
Breakfast		
Lunch		
Dinner		

Shipboard Activities

Excursion

Evening events _____

Attire _____

Favorite Memory _____

New Friends _____

Don't forget! _____

THINGS I WANT TO REMEMBER

Date _____

At Sea ○   Port ○   _____

Weather ☀ ☁ ☂ ❄   Temperature _____

	Restaurant	Menu Choice
Breakfast		
Lunch		
Dinner		

Shipboard Activities

Excursion

Evening events _____

Attire _____

Favorite Memory _____

New Friends _____

Don't forget! _____

THINGS I WANT TO REMEMBER

Date _____

At Sea ○   Port ○   _____

Weather ☀ ☁ ☂ ❄   Temperature _____

	Restaurant	Menu Choice
Breakfast		
Lunch		
Dinner		

Shipboard Activities

Excursion

Evening events _____

Attire _____

Favorite Memory _____

New Friends _____

Don't forget! _____

THINGS I WANT TO REMEMBER

Date _____

At Sea ○   Port ○   _____

Weather ☀ ☁ ☂ ❄   Temperature _____

	Restaurant	Menu Choice
Breakfast		
Lunch		
Dinner		

Shipboard Activities

Excursion

Evening events _____

Attire _____

Favorite Memory _____

New Friends _____

Don't forget! _____

STICK YOUR MEMORABILIA HERE

STICK YOUR MEMORABILIA HERE

Date: _____

At Sea ○   Port ○   _____

Weather ☀ ☁ ☂ ❄   Temperature _____

	Restaurant	Menu Choice
Breakfast		
Lunch		
Dinner		

Shipboard Activities

Excursion

Evening events _____

Attire _____

Favorite Memory _____

New Friends _____

Don't forget! _____

Date _____

At Sea ○   Port ○   _____

Weather ☀ ☁ ☂ ❄   Temperature _____

	Restaurant	Menu Choice
Breakfast		
Lunch		
Dinner		

Shipboard Activities

Excursion

Evening events _____

Attire _____

Favorite Memory _____

New Friends _____

Don't forget! _____

Date _____

At Sea ○   Port ○   _____

Weather ☀ ☁ ☂ ❄   Temperature _____

	Restaurant	Menu Choice
Breakfast		
Lunch		
Dinner		

Shipboard Activities

Excursion

Evening events _____

Attire _____

Favorite Memory _____

New Friends _____

Don't forget! _____

Date _____

At Sea ○   Port ○   _____

Weather ☀ ☁ ☂ ❄   Temperature _____

	Restaurant	Menu Choice
Breakfast		
Lunch		
Dinner		

Shipboard Activities

Excursion

Evening events _____

Attire _____

Favorite Memory _____

New Friends _____

Don't forget! _____

Date _____

At Sea ○   Port ○   _____

Weather ☀ ☁ ☂ ❄   Temperature _____

	Restaurant	Menu Choice
Breakfast		
Lunch		
Dinner		

Shipboard Activities

Excursion

Evening events _____

Attire _____

Favorite Memory _____

New Friends _____

Don't forget! _____

STICK YOUR MEMORABILIA HERE

STICK YOUR MEMORABILIA HERE

Date: _____

At Sea ○   Port ○   _____

Weather ☀ ☁ ☂ ❄   Temperature _____

	Restaurant	Menu Choice
Breakfast		
Lunch		
Dinner		

Shipboard Activities

Excursion

Evening events _____

Attire _____

Favorite Memory _____

New Friends _____

Don't forget! _____

Date _____

At Sea ○   Port ○   _____

Weather ☀ ☁ ☂ ❄   Temperature _____

	Restaurant	Menu Choice
Breakfast		
Lunch		
Dinner		

Shipboard Activities

Excursion

Evening events _____

Attire _____

Favorite Memory _____

New Friends _____

Don't forget! _____

Date: _____

At Sea ○   Port ○   _____

Weather ☀ ☁ ☂ ❄   Temperature _____

	Restaurant	Menu Choice
Breakfast		
Lunch		
Dinner		

Shipboard Activities

Excursion

Evening events _____

Attire _____

Favorite Memory _____

New Friends _____

Don't forget! _____

Date _____

At Sea ◯   Port ◯   _____

Weather ☀ ☁ ☂ ❄   Temperature _____

	Restaurant	Menu Choice
Breakfast		
Lunch		
Dinner		

Shipboard Activities

Excursion

Evening events _____

Attire _____

Favorite Memory _____

New Friends _____

Don't forget! _____

STICK YOUR MEMORABILIA HERE

STICK YOUR MEMORABILIA HERE

Date _____

At Sea ○   Port ○   _____

Weather ☀ ☁ ☂ ❄   Temperature _____

	Restaurant	Menu Choice
Breakfast		
Lunch		
Dinner		

Shipboard Activities

Excursion

Evening events _____

Attire _____

Favorite Memory _____

New Friends _____

Don't forget! _____

Date _____

At Sea ○   Port ○   _____

Weather ☀ ☁ ☂ ❄   Temperature _____

	Restaurant	Menu Choice
Breakfast		
Lunch		
Dinner		

Shipboard Activities

Excursion

Evening events _____

Attire _____

Favorite Memory _____

New Friends _____

Don't forget! _____

Date: _____

At Sea ○   Port ○   _____

Weather ☀ ☁ ☂ ❄   Temperature _____

	Restaurant	Menu Choice
Breakfast		
Lunch		
Dinner		

Shipboard Activities

Excursion

Evening events _____

Attire _____

Favorite Memory _____

New Friends _____

Don't forget! _____

Date _____

At Sea ○   Port ○   _____

Weather ☀ ☁ ☂ ❄   Temperature _____

	Restaurant	Menu Choice
Breakfast		
Lunch		
Dinner		

Shipboard Activities

Excursion

Evening events _____

Attire _____

Favorite Memory _____

New Friends _____

Don't forget! _____

Date _____

At Sea ○ Port ○ _____

Weather ☀ ☁ ☂ ❄   Temperature _____

	Restaurant	Menu Choice
Breakfast		
Lunch		
Dinner		

Shipboard Activities

Excursion

Evening events _____

Attire _____

Favorite Memory _____

New Friends _____

Don't forget! _____

STICK YOUR MEMORABILIA HERE

STICK YOUR MEMORABILIA HERE

Date _____

At Sea ○ Port ○ _____

Weather ☀ ☁ ☂ ❄   Temperature _____

	Restaurant	Menu Choice
Breakfast		
Lunch		
Dinner		

Shipboard Activities

Excursion

Evening events _____

Attire _____

Favorite Memory _____

New Friends _____

Don't forget! _____

Date _____

At Sea ○   Port ○   _____

Weather ☀ ☁ ☂ ❄   Temperature _____

	Restaurant	Menu Choice
Breakfast		
Lunch		
Dinner		

Shipboard Activities

Excursion

Evening events _____

Attire _____

Favorite Memory _____

New Friends _____

Don't forget! _____

Date _____

At Sea ○ Port ○ _____

Weather ☀ ☁ ☂ ❄   Temperature _____

	Restaurant	Menu Choice
Breakfast		
Lunch		
Dinner		

Shipboard Activities

Excursion

Evening events _____

Attire _____

Favorite Memory _____

New Friends _____

Don't forget! _____

Date _____

At Sea ○   Port ○   _____

Weather ☀ ☁ ☂ ❄   Temperature _____

	Restaurant	Menu Choice
Breakfast		
Lunch		
Dinner		

Shipboard Activities

Excursion

Evening events _____

Attire _____

Favorite Memory _____

New Friends _____

Don't forget! _____

Date _____

At Sea ○   Port ○ _____

Weather ☀ ☁ ☂ ❄   Temperature _____

	Restaurant	Menu Choice
Breakfast		
Lunch		
Dinner		

Shipboard Activities   Excursion

Evening events _____

Attire _____

Favorite Memory _____

New Friends _____

Don't forget! _____

STICK YOUR MEMORABILIA HERE

STICK YOUR MEMORABILIA HERE

Date _____

At Sea ○   Port ○   _____

Weather ☀ ☁ ☂ ❄   Temperature _____

	Restaurant	Menu Choice
Breakfast		
Lunch		
Dinner		

Shipboard Activities

Excursion

Evening events _____

Attire _____

Favorite Memory _____

New Friends _____

Don't forget! _____

Date _____

At Sea ○   Port ○   _____

Weather ☀ ☁ ☂ ❄   Temperature _____

	Restaurant	Menu Choice
Breakfast		
Lunch		
Dinner		

Shipboard Activities

Excursion

Evening events _____

Attire _____

Favorite Memory _____

New Friends _____

Don't forget! _____

Date _____

At Sea ○　Port ○　_____

Weather　☀ ☁ ☂ ❄　　　Temperature _____

	Restaurant	Menu Choice
Breakfast		
Lunch		
Dinner		

Shipboard Activities

Excursion

Evening events _____

Attire _____

Favorite Memory _____

New Friends _____

Don't forget! _____

Date _____

At Sea ○   Port ○   _____

Weather ☀ ☁ ☂ ❄   Temperature _____

	Restaurant	Menu Choice
Breakfast		
Lunch		
Dinner		

Shipboard Activities

Excursion

Evening events _____

Attire _____

Favorite Memory _____

New Friends _____

Don't forget! _____

Date _____

At Sea ○ Port ○ _____

Weather ☀ ☁ ☂ ❄   Temperature _____

	Restaurant	Menu Choice
Breakfast		
Lunch		
Dinner		

Shipboard Activities

Excursion

Evening events _____

Attire _____

Favorite Memory _____

New Friends _____

Don't forget! _____

STICK YOUR MEMORABILIA HERE

STICK YOUR MEMORABILIA HERE

Date _____

At Sea ○   Port ○   _____

Weather ☀ ☁ ☂ ❄   Temperature _____

	Restaurant	Menu Choice
Breakfast		
Lunch		
Dinner		

Shipboard Activities

Excursion

Evening events _____

Attire _____

Favorite Memory _____

New Friends _____

Don't forget! _____

Date _____

At Sea ○   Port ○

Weather ☀ ☁ ☂ ❄   Temperature _____

	Restaurant	Menu Choice
Breakfast		
Lunch		
Dinner		

Shipboard Activities

Excursion

Evening events _____

Attire _____

Favorite Memory _____

New Friends _____

Don't forget! _____

Date _____

At Sea ○ Port ○ _____

Weather ☀ ☁ ☂ ❄   Temperature _____

	Restaurant	Menu Choice
Breakfast		
Lunch		
Dinner		

Shipboard Activities

Excursion

Evening events _____

Attire _____

Favorite Memory _____

New Friends _____

Don't forget! _____

Date _____

At Sea ○   Port ○   _____

Weather ☀ ☁ ☂ ❄   Temperature _____

	Restaurant	Menu Choice
Breakfast		
Lunch		
Dinner		

Shipboard Activities

Excursion

Evening events _____

Attire _____

Favorite Memory _____

New Friends _____

Don't forget! _____

Date _____

At Sea ○   Port ○   _____

Weather ☀ ☁ ☂ ❄   Temperature _____

	Restaurant	Menu Choice
Breakfast		
Lunch		
Dinner		

Shipboard Activities

Excursion

Evening events _____

Attire _____

Favorite Memory _____

New Friends _____

Don't forget! _____

STICK YOUR MEMORABILIA HERE

STICK YOUR MEMORABILIA HERE

STICK YOUR MEMORABILIA HERE

STICK YOUR MEMORABILIA HERE

NOTES

NOTES

NOTES

NOTES

NOTES

NOTES

NOTES

NOTES

© 2019 by synexcellence publishing
info@synexcellence.com
c/o RA Stephan Schrage
Gneisenaustrasse 2a – 10961 Berlin
Germany

Printed in Great Britain
by Amazon